Have Colourful Dreams, Sir

by
Masoud Shakarami

translated by
Kioomars Ghanbari Azar

This first edition published in Australia in 2018 by:

Prahran Publishing
P.O. Box 2041, Prahran, Victoria, 3181

© Copyright Masoud Shakarami 2018

Masoud Shakarami has asserted his legal and moral right under the Copyright Act 1968 to be identified as the author of this work.

Published by arrangement with
Prahran Publishing, Australia.

All rights are strictly reserved.

No part of this publication may be reproduced, stored in a retrieval system or transmitted, in any form or by any other means, without the publisher's prior permission in writing. Copying of this script for performance reasons is also strictly prohibited by law, either in whole or excerpts from.

This book is sold subject to the condition that it shall not, by way of trade or otherwise, be lent, resold, hired out or otherwise circulated without the publisher's prior consent in any form of binding or cover other than that in which it is published and without similar condition, including this condition, being imposed on the subsequent purchaser.

Every reasonable effort has been made to trace copyright holders of material reproduced in this book, but if any have been inadvertently overlooked the publishers would be glad to hear from them. The story, all names, characters, and incidents portrayed in this book are fictitious. No identification with actual persons past or present, places, buildings, and products is intended or should be inferred.

```
ISBN 978-0-648-2040-4-6 eBook
ISBN 978-0-992-5069-9-5 Paperback
ISBN 978-0-648-2040-0-8 Script
```

Dewey: 792.1

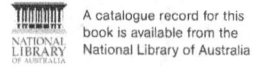

A catalogue record for this book is available from the National Library of Australia

Performance Licensing and Royalty Payments

Masoud Shakarami retains control of both the amateur and professional stage performance rights of this play. No unauthorised performance should occur without the express and written permission of the author. Royalty payments for performances may be coordinated through the publisher - Prahran Publishing.

Restriction of Alteration

There shall be no modifications of any kind to the play including deletion of dialogue (including objectionable language), changes to characters gender or names, title of the play or music without the express and written permission from the author.

Publisher Attribution

All advertising and printed amaterial connected with the performance must include the following notice:

Produced by special arrangement with
Prahran Publishing (www.prahran.press)

Sound and Video Recordings

This play may contain stage directions to include the use of music, video or other sound recordings either in part or in whole. The author and the publisher have not sought the right to use such content and performance rights permission should be obtained seperately. Permission to record audio and video recordings of all performances must also be explicitly given by the author in writing.

Author Credit

Performance rights approval requires credit be given to Masoud Shakarami as the sole and exclusive author of the play. This obligation applies to the title page of every program or other advertising material distributed in connection to this play. The author's credit should appear immediately under the title of the play on all published material, and alongside no other individual. Font size of credit cannot be less than 50% of the largest letter used in the play's title.

Please email info@prahran.press
for all performance enquiries.

Front Cover: Two Lovers
Painted in 1630 by Reza Abbasi
Courtesy of Wikimedia Commons [Public domain]

Calligraphy Artwork by:
Sajjad Mofrad-Taheri

Back Cover Photographed by:
Siamak Adib

Have Colourful Dreams, Sir

By Masoud Shakarami

This book is dedicated to my beloved mother
Nahid Mobasheri

There is no barrier between the lover and the beloved

The barrier is only thyself

Hafez, begone

Awards and Nominations:

2016: Best Iranian Actor of the Year, Nominee

2016: Winner Best Playwright, Fajr International Theatre Festival 1st Place

2013: Best Playwright, Hamedan International Theatre Festival, 2rd Place

2011: Best Playwright, Hamedan International Theatre Festival, 3rd Place

2010: Best Actor, Iranian National Youth Festival, 2nd Place

http://masoudshakarami.actor

About the Author

MASOUD SHAKARAMI, the Playwright and the Play *Have Colourful Dreams, Sir*.

Masoud Shakarami (1986 - Tehran, Iran), has a BA in dramatic literature, worked as playwright, director and actor since 2006 and has been nominated and won several awards as a playwright and actor.

Masoud's study has focused on mythology and mythological literature.

> "I think my play deserves to be noticed and considered by anyone who is interested in eastern love stories. It is all about love. Eastern love is something so strange and painful. The philosophy of eastern love is to withstand the pain of separation and to surrender everything to the beloved, even life."

Introduction

Have Colourful Dreams, Sir is a dramatic reflection of the quality and characteristics of classic Persian lyricism. The play draws upon the content and structure of a Lyrical Poem in literature. A *Ghazal* (The Persian word for Lyrical Poem) means making love and speaking with a beloved in an aggrandised romantic language. This poetic form first emerged in Iranian literature in the 10th – 11th century and blossomed around the 13th and 14th century with the revered poets and philosophers such as *Saadi* and *Hafez*.

A *Ghazal* has 10 to 15 verses, and each verse contains complete and independent content and meaning within itself. One of the most important things about a *Ghazal* is its mutual, common and repeated subjects, such as:

The Lover: (The "LAME" in the play):

He is usually a weak, languished man who can do many wondrous things. He can change the order of the universe, move mountains, and do almost anything, but only if his beloved desires it so. His only weakness is love itself. The only thing he gains from love is pain. The more he falls in love with his beloved, he gradually becomes further from his true self until he loses his identity completely.

The Beloved ("NEGAR" in the play):

Negar is a common word for the beloved in Iranian Lyricism and is also a romantic female name for Persian girls. The primary goal for the beloved is to seduce the Lover. She is the reason for the Lover's pain, yet she sympathises and commiserates him. It's Complicated.

The Love:

The relationship between the Lover and the Beloved is fraught with difficulties. This profound and intricate relationship is called love. In classic Persian Lyricism, the Lover and the beloved never truly unite because love is love only in separation. Physically realising that love means nothing. The poem gives no reason for this separation, and of course, no one asks for it.

There is a firm belief that love in Iranian Poetry, is a symbol of a super humanistic love between Man and God and no man can get to God without becoming dissolved in Him. If you look at this in some humanistic way, it would seem a real tragedy, but to a Mystic, it is all joy and happiness: a spiritual complication.

Insufficient Information:

In a *Ghazal*, the poet never gives complete information to the reader, for such reasons as:

First, they believe that the reader is himself a person in love, and knows everything necessary to understand the Lyrics, so there is no need to waste time in explanation (or perhaps to be economical with words due to the 10 to 15 verse limit).

Second, the reader who is also in love is a dreamer and illusionist who can quickly fill in the blanks. In other words, the reader is a creative artist, not a child that needs only to enjoy a story and say good night. The Reader, because of his power of creation and imagination, must contemplate the poem, enlighten its darker points and interpret the symbols and metaphors for his or herself. A Persian *Ghazal* is the poem of creation, imagination, philosophy and interpretation. Anytime you read a *Ghazal*, you will come to understand and become enlightened about eras long since past.

All of that said, this introduction is not a key to the understanding of Persian Poetry, but an illumination into absorbing this play more smoothly. There is only one way to understand a *Ghazal*, and it is not to study it for years, nor visiting various countries nor becoming familiar with the great poets. To understand *Ghazal*, you only have to drink wine and fall in LOVE.

~Masoud Shakarami

CHARACTERS

LAME:	A handsome young crippled man.
NEGAR:	A beautiful young woman.
SHAMAN:	An elderly mystic man.
COOKIE COOK:	A large elderly lady baker of magical cookies.
PARIA:	A young woman.
FRIEND:	A brash young man
FRIEND'S WIFE:	A cynical young woman.
GIRL:	Naive young lady.
NEXT GIRL:	Another naive young lady.

3 Male + 6 Female

Act I

SCENE 1

After a funeral. All characters [Lame, Shaman, Cookie Cook, Friend, Friend's Wife and Paria along with some other people] are eating. They are all dressed in black.

FRIEND:	I think it was the most stupid death I have ever seen.
SHAMAN:	You're wrong.
FRIEND:	No. It really was the most stupid death I have ever seen.
C.C.:	Have some respect, please.
FRIEND:	OK. But admit it, that was a very weird death.
SHAMAN:	It wasn't.
FRIEND:	It wasn't? Someone's dead from joy... Isn't that really weird?
SHAMAN:	He did such crazy things after Paria left him, so it wasn't weird that he'd die from joy when she returned.
C.C.:	Would you like to talk about something else?
FRIEND:	I really wouldn't.
SHAMAN:	I also think we had better change the subject.

FRIEND:	I won't stop wondering, even if you change the subject.
FRIEND'S WIFE:	Can you just stop wondering. Please?
FRIEND:	Someone realises, that after three years, his lover *(Pointing at Paria)* is coming back from her journey...
C.C.:	*(Interrupts him)* Why don't you continue your argument at your house?
FRIEND:	Why do you insist we stop arguing?
SHAMAN:	*(A little upset)* Because we expect you to appreciate that this woman *(Pointing at Paria)* and the rest of us are in mourning.
PARIA:	*(Sobbing)* Let him continue, Shaman.
FRIEND:	I didn't mean to hurt you, Paria.
PARIA:	My sorrow is so much more than this.
FRIEND'S WIFE:	I apologise too.
PARIA:	There's no need. But don't you think that it is a little too soon?

Act I Scene 1

SHAMAN: *(Sardonically)* Yes, I also think that just two hours after the funeral is a little soon.

FRIEND: I apologise again.

Everyone continues eating in silence; Paria cries.

C.C.: *(Joyfully tries to change the mood)* I have a suggestion. Would you like to put this situation behind us? We could become just as we were before.

SHAMAN: Why not? Sorrow and sadness are becoming apparent, aren't they? *(Silence)* Has anyone on this island previously had any sorrow or sadness? *(They all deny having any)* So why don't you all believe me when I say there should absolutely be no sorrow nor sadness?

FRIEND: We don't have a problem with that but...

They all look at Paria who is crying.

SHAMAN: *(Doesn't know what to say)* Well... Ah... Well... I think there's only one little problem...

PARIA:	It's not a little problem.
SHAMAN:	Yes. You're right. It isn't… But something has to be done about it… *(Paria continues crying)*
LAME:	*(Who has been eating in silence from the beginning)* Paria.
PARIA:	Yes?
LAME:	Throw your sorrow and sadness away and don't cry anymore.
	People on this island need you… Don't they?
PARIA:	Yes…
LAME:	So, stop crying and let us all be happy again.
PARIA:	OK… Sure.
LAME:	Thank you.
PARIA:	*(Smiling)* That was very kind of you, Lame. I was actually feeling really really bad.
LAME:	It's OK.

Act I Scene 1

PARIA: Cookie Cook, could you please make some cookies for us tonight, so that we can forget our sorrow and sadness and celebrate?

C.C.: Sure. What kind of cookies would you like?

SHAMAN: Walnut cookies.

FRIEND: Coconut cookies.

FRIEND'S WIFE: I prefer a simple cookie.

PARIA: I agree with Shaman. Walnut cookies, please.

LAME: I like almond cookies.

SHAMAN: So, we'll have almond cookies tonight.

C.C.: *(Laughing to Shaman)* You didn't think I'd make walnut cookies for you, did you?

They all laugh.

Just eat your lunch. We should get ready for tonight.

PARIA:	*(Smiling to Lame)* I wish you had comforted me sooner. I was nearly grief-stricken to death. Losing him is really hard for me.
LAME:	*(Solemnly joking)* No. We needed a little sadness.

Everybody laughs; The Shaman is thinking.

	What are you thinking about Shaman?
FRIEND:	I hope you're still thinking that someone has actually died from joy.
SHAMAN:	I told you, I don't care about that.
FRIEND:	Don't you? Why?
SHAMAN:	You know what? I am thinking about that.
FRIEND:	So how can you say that you don't care about it?
SHAMAN::	I'm looking at it from a different point of view.
FRIEND::	What do you mean?

Act I Scene 1

SHAMAN:	When Paria came back, he died of joy. That means that he really loved her. So it's not strange that he died of joy. But why didn't he die from sadness when Paria left him?
FRIEND:	That makes it even more weird.
SHAMAN:	Yes, it does. But it makes his staying alive weird, not his death.
LAME:	It's not important anymore.
SHAMAN:	I agree.
C.C.:	So do I.
LAME:	Let's change the subject. It's better this way.
C.C.:	Who has almonds at home?
FRIEND:	We do.
FRIEND'S WIFE:	He's right, we do.
PARIA:	Can I bring the almonds?
SHAMAN:	Lame likes me to bring the almonds for the cookies.
LAME:	*(Smiling)* I would like C.C. to bring the almonds herself.
SHAMAN:	Yes, that's a better idea.

C.C.: *(To Lame)* Thank you very much.

LAME: But we will all help you cook.

FRIEND'S WIFE: *(Has finished her lunch; to Friend)* Shall we go?

FRIEND: Where?... What happened?

FRIEND'S WIFE: I want to get ready for tonight. Get up now.

PARIA: She's right. I should go get prepared too.

LAME: See you all tonight. *(Excitedly)* Don't forget the pomegranate juice. *(Sudden silence)* What? Why are you all looking at me like that? *(No one speaks)* Are almond cookies with pomegranate juice such a strange thing? *(No one speaks)* Shaman, is it so?

SHAMAN: *(Stammering)* Well... Ah... No, it's not... But... You know?... If you have those things...

LAME: You mean, I may lose my hair? *(The Shaman nods his head)* Well, who cares? It'll grow back again. *(Laughs)* It's worth doing, isn't it?

Act I Scene 1

SHAMAN: There's no way you'll change your mind?

LAME: Not at all. Because I've really had a craving for pomegranate juice.

SHAMAN: *(Excitedly)* So then, we'll have it.

Everybody laughs

FRIEND: Thank God. So, let's go home now. And this time, we will take Lame home.

PARIA: No, it's my turn.

LAME: Don't start that again. I'll go to C.C.'s house and help her cook the cookies.

PARIA: I'll bring the pomegranate juice. Shall I?

LAME: *(Smiling)* OK, you can do that.

PARIA: *(Very happy)* Thank you.

SCENE 2

All characters except Lame are present. They are carrying dishes of food with them.

PARIA: I've made some stew for him… Let me take it to him today.

C.C.: He doesn't like stew very much.

PARIA: Yes, he does. I've taken stew to him before.

SHAMAN: Why bother making stew at all? I've brought some kebab for him.

(Sardonically) I think kebab is more delicious than stew.

PARIA: This stew is different.

SHAMAN: Why?

FRIEND: Perhaps you've made it with lamb, Paria. Huh? *(Laughs along with his wife)*

PARIA: No, but I've really made a lot of effort with it.

FRIEND'S WIFE: Well, we've really put in a lot of effort with our food as well.

SHAMAN: Lame really likes lamb, doesn't he? *(Everyone nods)*

	So, if there is some lamb in that stew, then I'll concede.
PARIA:	But... It cannot be. You say such weird things, Shaman.
SHAMAN:	You didn't use lamb in your stew and Lame likes lamb very much.
PARIA:	But...
SHAMAN:	But lamb can be used in kebab.
PARIA:	What do you mean?
SHAMAN:	I've made kebab for him. So, I think it's better that I take it to him.
C.C.:	That's not a good reason at all.
SHAMAN:	Why not?
C.C.:	Everybody knows that Lame likes cookies the most.
FRIEND'S WIFE:	And you want to take cookies to him?
C.C.:	Yes, I do.
FRIEND:	Even if he does like cookies, I don't think he wants to eat them today. Especially for his lunch.
C.C.:	Why not?

Act I Scene 2

FRIEND'S WIFE:	It's obvious. Because he had a lot of cookies and pomegranate juice the other night during the celebration.
C.C.:	That's not a good reason.
SHAMAN:	She's right... It's not a good reason that he wouldn't have cookies because he had cookies last night.
C.C.:	Thank you, Shaman.
SHAMAN:	You're welcome. But he may feel ill if he eats too many cookies.
FRIEND:	*(Laughs loudly; to The Shaman)* Well done. Excellent.
SHAMAN:	*(Tries to hide his laughter)* What was excellent?
FRIEND:	*(Changes the subject)* Nothing. You haven't made your kebab by sorcery, have you?
SHAMAN:	No. Honest. I have really made it myself.
FRIEND'S WIFE:	Just like us.
SHAMAN:	But the lamb I used, was enchanted. It's certainly beneficial for him.
FRIEND:	And then again, maybe it's not.

SHAMAN: Of course it is.

PARIA: Please let me take the stew to him.

SHAMAN: But kebab is more delicious.

C.C.: Cookies are.

FRIEND: I disagree.

PARIA: What have you made yourself?

FRIEND: We've made some kind of bake that no one's ever had before.

SHAMAN: Objection. It may hurt him.

FRIEND: How can a bake hurt someone?

SHAMAN: Remember that he's a Lame. He loses his hair when he drinks pomegranate juice.

FRIEND'S WIFE: There's no pomegranate juice in our bake.

SHAMAN: Don't you listen to me? A Lame's body is totally different to a normal body. Every single minute something unpredictable may happen to him which we know nothing about.

Act I Scene 2

FRIEND'S WIFE: We've put lamb, pumpkin, salt, some spicy vegetables and a little pepper in it.

SHAMAN: What kind of pepper?

FRIEND'S WIFE: Red pepper.

SHAMAN: That's ok. Red pepper doesn't cause any problems.

FRIEND: We wanted to bring Lame's food and add a little variety today.

C.C.: 'Variety?' How?

FRIEND: Simply by bringing a new bake to him.

C.C.: I must say that's not a bad idea.

SHAMAN: I agree.

FRIEND: Really?

SHAMAN: Yes, I agree.

C.C.: So do I.

FRIEND: I really appreciate it.

C.C.: We must do something about this situation.

FRIEND'S WIFE: What 'situation'?

C.C.:	This situation. Who should bring the food, who should bring the clothes, who should do this, who should do that.
FRIEND:	I agree.
SHAMAN:	So do I. Except the special conditions, of course.
FRIEND:	I agree.
PARIA:	I don't agree.
FRIEND'S WIFE:	What do you mean?
PARIA:	Well, I want him to have my stew.
FRIEND'S WIFE:	We all agree. You agree, please.
PARIA:	I don't agree.
FRIEND'S WIFE:	Please, Paria.
PARIA:	I can't.
SHAMAN:	Paria. You want to take your stew to Lame to make him happy, don't you?
PARIA:	Yes.
SHAMAN:	We are trying to take the best dish for him to enjoy. Him, not us.

Act I Scene 2

PARIA: So why are you all fighting about taking your own dishes to him?

SHAMAN: Because we all thought that our own dish was the best, but now we agree that this bake is the best dish.

PARIA: So, what should I do with my stew?

SHAMAN: You can eat it yourself. Just like my kebab. But only the best dish is taken to Lame. OK?

PARIA: Yes then...

SHAMAN: ...then you can change your stew for my kebab. *(Laughs)*

SCENE 3

Lame's place. Friend and his wife have brought the bake to Lame. Lame has lost all his hair.

FRIEND: Eat. Nothing will go wrong.

LAME: *(Jokingly)* Are you sure? Is there some pomegranate juice in it?

FRIEND'S WIFE: No. Relax. I've made it myself.

FRIEND: We spoke with Shaman about it. We told him what's in it.

LAME: And?

FRIEND: Nothing. He said that you can eat it without a problem.

LAME: I have no more hair to lose anyway. But then again, it may hurt me somewhere else.

FRIEND: Why do you feel so queasy today?

LAME: Because of the other night's pomegranate juice.

FRIEND: We told you not to drink it, but you did anyway.

FRIEND'S WIFE: It's not important anymore. Your hair will grow back.

FRIEND:	It's important that today you're going to have my wife's cuisine once again.

Silence. Lame looks at them.

LAME:	Do you like her cuisine?
FRIEND:	Yes. Why do you ask?
LAME:	What about her? Do you love your wife?
FRIEND:	More than my very eyes.
LAME:	*(To the Wife)* Do you love him too?
FRIEND'S WIFE:	More than the entire world. Why are you asking these questions?
LAME:	Do you go walking along the coast together at sunset?
FRIEND:	Has something happened?
LAME:	Just answer my question.
FRIEND:	Well… Yes… Some days we go walking along the coast at sunset. Like most couples living on the Island.
LAME:	Sometimes I go to the coast at sunset.

Act I Scene 3

FRIEND'S WIFE: I haven't seen you there.

LAME: I watch from a distance.

 When you come to a cliff, do you sit together and watch the sea?

FRIEND: No.

LAME: No?

FRIEND: We just like to take each other's hand and walk. We don't like to sit.

FRIEND'S WIFE: Sometimes, I like to throw stones in the water.

FRIEND: *(To his wife)* We both do.

FRIEND'S WIFE: *(To her husband, complaining)* Only 'sometimes'.

LAME: How old are you?

FRIEND: Twenty-six.

LAME: I'm twenty-eight.

FRIEND: Do you want to tell me what's happened?

LAME: No.

FRIEND'S WIFE: Tell us. If there's something wrong, we'll do everything we can for you.

LAME:	I know you will.
FRIEND'S WIFE:	So, tell us what's happened.
LAME:	No.
FRIEND:	I'm your friend. I must know.
LAME:	There's no need. Yet.
FRIEND:	Yet? You are making us worry.
LAME:	Thank you for the bake.
FRIEND:	But we…
LAME:	Do not ask anymore.
FRIEND'S WIFE:	It will be delicious if you pour a little lemon juice on it.
LAME:	Thanks.
FRIEND'S WIFE:	I didn't add it myself. The lemon juice is in that bottle. I thought you might like to add it yourself.
LAME:	Thanks again.
FRIEND:	OK. We should leave. Goodbye now.
LAME:	Could you ask your wife to leave us alone for a moment?

The Wife exits.

LAME:	It's been a long time since I have felt anything. I don't think I can tolerate it.
	I will tell you.
FRIEND:	That's very kind of you. By the way, may I have a guess?
LAME:	I don't think you can...
FRIEND:	Yes, I think I can.
LAME:	Just Go! Don't let your wife be alone.

SCENE 4

The people of the Island have gathered; They are obviously worried.

FRIEND: You should've been absolutely sure about this.

SHAMAN: Almost sure.

FRIEND: Almost?

SHAMAN: He hasn't said anything yet.

FRIEND'S WIFE: He has talked the same way to all ten couples who have come to visit him.

PARIA: What should we do now?

SHAMAN: We should make sure.

PARIA: And then? We can't do anything about it, can we?

SHAMAN: *(Sardonically)* These days all people on this Island have the same problem and we cannot do anything about it.

PARIA: We can talk to him...

SHAMAN: *(Doesn't care about what Paria says)* I think we should first make sure and then decide.

FRIEND:	*(To C.C.)* Don't you want to say something?
C.C.:	I'm thinking.
FRIEND:	About that how weird it is that someone dies from joy after his love returns to him? *(Laughs)*
SHAMAN:	Do you not understand? This is not a good time for jokes.
FRIEND:	*(Apologetically)* But it's really weird to me.
C.C.:	Please. We are not in a good situation.
FRIEND:	I'm sorry. Continue.
SHAMAN:	We should be sure, somehow.
PARIA:	How?
SHAMAN:	I don't know. Maybe we should ask him directly.
C.C.:	Not a good idea.
SHAMAN:	Why not?
C.C.:	Because if we ask him directly, then he will ask us directly.

SHAMAN: *(Disappointed)* It sounds like we may have to find him one.

FRIEND: But we can't.

C.C.: Exactly. We can't.

FRIEND: So then, it's not a good idea.

FRIEND'S WIFE: But we can't just sit and do nothing, can we?

SHAMAN: No. But there must be a way.

FRIEND'S WIFE: You know, I pity him a little.

PARIA: Maybe much more than 'a little'.

FRIEND'S WIFE: *(Begging)* Please, do something.

C.C.: What? We're not even sure about it.

FRIEND: Why not? It's obvious.

SHAMAN: I still think that we had better go ask him.

C.C.: Why should we do that? Considering we already know. Considering that we can't do anything about it. Considering that he might ask us to...

SHAMAN:	*(Interrupts her)* We should make sure. So that we are able to make the best decision. To confident as to what we should do next.
FRIEND:	I agree.
FRIEND'S WIFE:	So do I.
PARIA:	Do you want me to ask him?
FRIEND:	He wouldn't confide in you.
FRIEND'S WIFE:	Yes. He wouldn't.
SHAMAN:	Do you want me to read his mind?
C.C.:	You think you can do that?
SHAMAN:	Yes. But I don't think it's good to read Lame's mind.
C.C.:	That is exactly why I asked.
PARIA:	So, what should we do? To get answers?
C.C.:	He might tell me.
SHAMAN:	We can try that.
C.C.:	I'll ask him myself.
SHAMAN:	Take some walnut cookies and cream to him. It will benefit his hair.

SCENE 5

Lame's place. Lame is eating walnut cookies and cream.

C.C.:	You like it?
LAME:	Very much.
C.C.:	It's a walnut cookie.
LAME:	I love walnut cookies.
C.C.:	I wanted to bring almond cookies to you at first, but Shaman said that walnut cookies along with the cream would benefit your hair. It'll make it grow again.
LAME:	I don't like almonds.
C.C.:	I knew that. But the other night you asked for almond cookies. I told myself 'Lame is really strange'.
LAME:	It was because they were all calling out different cookies. I wanted to ask for a cookie which they hadn't mentioned. I wanted to spite them. *(Both laugh)*
C.C.:	Have some cream too. Your hair will grow faster.
LAME:	Yes, of course I will.

C.C.:	That's good. Now, tell me this story.
LAME:	What story?
C.C.:	You mean you don't know what I'm talking about?
LAME:	Yes, I know.
C.C.:	So tell me what's wrong with you.
LAME:	You mean you don't know what's wrong with me?
C.C.:	We've guessed some things, but we're not sure yet.
LAME:	They've sent you to make sure?
C.C.:	Yes. *(Short silence)*
LAME:	I need a wife. *(C.C. is shocked)* I long to love someone. Go walking with her at sunset, *(Remembers that he cannot walk and corrects himself)* sit on a cliff by the sea with her at sunset. Have a wife who likes to throw stones in the water. And we just do sometimes.
C.C.:	*(Suddenly starts crying and beating herself)* Until now I was telling myself that I was wrong. What the hell should we do now?

Act 1 Scene 5

LAME:	Cry, as much as you like.
C.C.:	*(Still crying)* How can we find a wife for you?
	Yell "Hey! People! Come here! We've got an offer you cannot refuse."
LAME:	Even if all the people of the Island come together, they cannot do anything about it.
C.C.:	Let them come, maybe we can figure out what the hell it is we should do.
LAME:	As you wish. So, tell them all to come here.
C.C.:	*(To the door)* Come in. Everybody gather around.

Shaman, Friend, Friend's Wife and Paria enter; All crying.

LAME:	You were listening?
SHAMAN:	We had to.
LAME:	Oh. That's nuts. Don't cry, for God's sake.

Everyone stops crying.

LAME:	OK. Now we can talk.
SHAMAN:	What can we talk about?
LAME:	What should we do now?
FRIEND:	We should find a woman for you.
LAME:	Then find one.
FRIEND'S WIFE:	But, how? *(Silence)*
LAME:	Have I ever asked for anything unnatural?
SHAMAN:	Never.
LAME:	This is the first time and I can't do anything about it.
C.C.:	Do you think we can?
LAME:	We need to find a solution.
SHAMAN:	I don't think there is a solution.
PARIA:	Why not?
SHAMAN:	Because there's no girl on this island, or perhaps anywhere in the world who can live with a Lame. It's impossible. Understand?
PARIA:	I know that, but I'm saying, maybe we can find a different solution.

Act I Scene 5

SHAMAN: What solution?

LAME: I am sorry. But I need it, and I cannot do anything to deny it.

Lame exits disappointed.

FRIEND: *(To C.C.)* Can't you cook him some more cookies and make him forget about marrying?

C.C.: We talked about this before.

I can, but it's not right.

FRIEND'S WIFE: I agree.

PARIA: *(To Friend's Wife)* Then you give us a solution.

FRIEND'S WIFE: I agree. He absolutely has the right to get married.

SHAMAN: We have no problem with him marrying but there is no Lame anywhere in the world who is deserving of our Lame.

PARIA: When I was off the island, I knew a girl who was Lame. Shall I bring her here?

SHAMAN: Did her people treat her like we treat our Lame?

PARIA:	No. She lived under a dank bridge. But people gave her food and water and clothes.
SHAMAN:	She's just an ordinary Lame. Like many others. We need a Lame like ours, not an ordinary one.
C.C.:	It sounds hopeless. I think we had better go home and think some more. Let's meet again later.
PARIA:	I agree.
FRIEND:	So do we.
SHAMAN:	I think I have to agree too.

Act II

SCENE 1

Lame's place. Lame and Friend are lying down. It seems that they have been in this position for hours. Lame's hair has fully grown. There is a mess around the room.

LAME: Aren't you going home? *(Friend gets up)* No, I meant... I meant if you think you should go, don't worry about me. Just go.

FRIEND: *(Lies down again)* I've got nothing else to do. I like staying here with you.

LAME: Your wife may worry.

FRIEND: I told her that I was coming to your place, so I told her to go to Paria's place.

LAME: Paria's place?

FRIEND: Yes. Why do you ask?

LAME: Nothing. Err, do you think Paria is a good girl?

FRIEND: Yes, I believe she is.

LAME: And she is beautiful.

FRIEND: But she's not Lame.

LAME:	I wish she was.
FRIEND:	Are you sad?
LAME:	Very.
FRIEND:	Do you wish you were healthy?
LAME:	Never.
FRIEND:	I knew you'd say that.
LAME:	If she was Lame… *(Stops talking)*
FRIEND:	Do you love her?
LAME:	No… Oh I don't know.
FRIEND:	It makes no difference.
LAME:	Maybe she still has feelings from her first relationship.
FRIEND:	That really was a stupid relationship.
LAME:	I don't know what to say.
FRIEND:	When I saw him fuss over everything, just before Paria's return and before his death, I didn't know whether I should laugh at him or pity him.
LAME:	His death didn't seem stupid to me.
FRIEND:	Why so?

LAME:	Dying from joy is much better than dying from illness, or falling off a cliff, or being eaten by a wolf, or bleeding to death, or for instance... falling from a bed while sleeping and then being hit on the head by the corner of a table and dying, or getting bitten by a snake, or...
FRIEND:	...OK. OK. I admit, it's a death full of pleasure, but it was still stupid.
LAME:	Do you think that dying from sorrow is also stupid?
FRIEND:	Of course not.
LAME:	I'm afraid I will die from sorrow.
FRIEND:	Take it easy. We will find a solution.
LAME:	I hope so.
FRIEND:	Back to Paria, believe me, she doesn't think about her previous relationship anymore.
LAME:	How do you know that?
FRIEND:	Because you asked her not to be sad anymore.
LAME:	Well then, that makes me happy.

FRIEND: I told you, it doesn't make any difference.

LAME: I mean it's great that someone's sadness has gone away. If I was the reason for Shaman, C.C. or anyone else to forget about their sadness, I'd feel happy.

FRIEND: I know. I was just joking.

LAME: I have to think. Maybe I can find a solution myself.

FRIEND: All the people on the Island are trying.

LAME: I know.

FRIEND: All the people but us. *(They both laugh)*

LAME: Go home now. Your wife is alone.

FRIEND: *(Gets up)* She's at Paria's place.

LAME: I need to think. Maybe there's a solution I haven't thought of yet.

SCENE 2

People of the Island have gathered.

C.C.:	Everything's going wrong. It can't be.
SHAMAN:	*(Impatiently)* What now?
FRIEND:	What should we do? We haven't found a solution.
C.C.:	It can't be. We have to find a woman for Lame.
FRIEND'S WIFE:	I have a suggestion, but I'm not too sure.
FRIEND:	Not a problem, darling, tell us.
FRIEND'S WIFE:	But I'm not sure it's such a good idea.
PARIA:	Tell us. It's better than nothing.
FRIEND'S WIFE:	I thought that maybe we had best get off the island, maybe we can find a Lame…
SHAMAN:	*(Upset)* We deserve being fooled.
FRIEND'S WIFE:	*(Confused)* "Fooled?" I didn't mean to fool anyone.
SHAMAN:	It was obvious.

FRIEND:	My wife just said what she thought...
C.C.:	...and it wasn't a bad...
SHAMAN:	Wasn't it?
C.C.:	The only way... is the best way...
SHAMAN:	It's not the only way...
FRIEND:	Do you know any other way?
SHAMAN:	*(Stammering)* Well, I, no, I do not.
FRIEND:	So this is the best way.
C.C.:	We should form teams.
SHAMAN:	Do what you want.
PARIA:	What is it, Shaman? Why are you so upset?
SHAMAN:	I'm not upset. I just...
PARIA:	*(Interrupts him)* So when are we forming teams?
C.C.:	The sooner, the better.
PARIA:	*(To Friend)* Can I be with you?
FRIEND:	Of course. We need everyone.
C.C.:	Shaman. Are you coming with us?
SHAMAN:	I'll go to the east with my team.

Act II Scene 2

C.C.: There are no teams yet.

SHAMAN: I'll take my group with me.

C.C.: I agree.

FRIEND'S WIFE: So do I.

FRIEND: Deal.

PARIA: *(To Shaman)* May I come with you?

SHAMAN: You?

PARIA: *(Smiling)* Please. I'm excited.

SHAMAN: *(Smiles)* OK. You can come with us.

FRIEND: We'll go west with our team.

FRIEND'S WIFE: With who?

FRIEND: Doesn't matter. We should gather everyone, then we can choose.

C.C.: I'll go south.

Lame enters suddenly:

LAME: There's no need anymore...

C.C.: What?

LAME: You don't have to go to the south. *(All become happy)*

C.C.:	*(Happy)* Why?
LAME:	I found a solution.
SHAMAN:	Excellent.
FRIEND:	What's your solution?
LAME:	It's concerning Shaman.
C.C.:	You mean... we should still go?
LAME:	It doesn't matter.
SHAMAN:	What should I do?
LAME:	Make a girl Lame for me.

Silence. All look at each other and don't move. Only Paria divulges her anguish. All look at her. She calms down.

SHAMAN:	What does that mean?
LAME:	Then there'll be another Lame who can be my wife.
PARIA:	Is that possible?
LAME:	The great Shaman with all his magic should answer that.
SHAMAN:	There may be a way... but... it is not good, usually.

LAME:	What do you mean?
SHAMAN:	We can make someone Lame, but it usually just makes her Lame, an ordinary Lame. I mean she cannot be your wife.
PARIA:	We can at least try, can't we?
SHAMAN:	Are you thinking of any particular girl?
LAME:	Does it make any difference?
SHAMAN:	Yes, it does. Because we should make several attempts. Maybe it works, maybe it doesn't.
LAME:	So, could someone please tell all the girls of the Island that if they want to marry me, they can participate in this trial?
PARIA:	Is it really necessary?
C.C.:	I say…
FRIEND:	*(To Lame)* Didn't you want to marry…?
LAME:	*(Interrupts him)* Please don't name anyone.
FRIEND:	OK. As you wish.

LAME: It would seem that we can't consider her, given what Shaman said.

FRIEND: But it doesn't make much of a difference. *(Lame and Friend laugh)*

LAME: *(Laughing)* Yes, it certainly doesn't.

SCENE 3

Many girls have gathered. There is a ceremony and joyful music is being played. The girls are very happy and toss flowers in the air. Among the girls, there is a girl named Negar. After a few moments, Lame, Shaman, C.C., Friend, Wife and some other people enter. The girls become silent.

SHAMAN: Dear girls. You all know why we've gathered here today. It is my responsibility to explain the situation. One of you is going to become Lame and who may be able to marry Lame *(Points to Lame)* I said 'maybe' because there might not be a turn for everyone and the first girl might become Lame the way need… But she also might not, and then it'd be the next girl's turn… and the next and the next. Any problems? *(Girls applaud and cheer)* OK. Let's start according to the list I've written. The first one step forward… *(One of the girls steps forward. Other girls applaud and cheer)* Are you ready?

THE GIRL: *(Excitedly)* Yes.

SHAMAN: Sit down.

THE GIRL:	God, help me.
NEGAR:	*(From the crowd, laughing)* I pray it doesn't work.
THE GIRL:	And I pray it does. Anyway, there's no chance for you. *(Both laugh)*
SHAMAN:	OK. Enough joking. Are you ready?
THE GIRL:	*(Sits in the Paralysing Chair)* Yes.

Shaman takes a bludgeon out of his bag.

NEGAR:	*(Jokingly)* Run! His bludgeon is so big.
THE GIRL:	*(Laughing)* Go ahead, I'll stay here and become his wife.
SHAMAN:	Silence. Are you ready?
The Girl	Yes. Yes, I'm ready. I'm ready. Do it for God's sake.

Shaman hits the girl in her back with the bludgeon. She falls to the ground. Shaman, Friend and C.C. gather around her quickly.

SHAMAN:	Move your feet. *(The Girl moves her feet)*
FRIEND:	It didn't work. Take another hit.

Shaman hits the girl repeatedly until she loses consciousness.

SHAMAN: I think she's become unconscious.

C.C.: Yes.

SHAMAN: Bring her back.

Friend's Wife pours some water on the girl's face and she suddenly wakens.

SHAMAN: Can you move your feet?

The girl tries but cannot move her feet. She screams with joy, yet she feels weak.

THE GIRL: No. I can't. *(To Negar)* Didn't I tell you it'd be me?

SHAMAN: *(Inspects feet)* It didn't work. Next one. *(Girls applaud and cheer)*

NEGAR: *(To the Girl)* Didn't I tell you, it wouldn't?

THE GIRL: *(Laughing sarcastically)* I hope it won't be you either.

NEGAR: Don't be hopeful, my dear.

They get the girl out of the 'Paralysing Chair' as Shaman ordered. All cheer for her.

SHAMAN:	I'll try a different method. Next one please. *(The next girl steps forward)* Are you ready, my dear?
NEXT GIRL:	Yes.
SHAMAN:	*(Sarcastically to Negar)* Are you sure you don't you want to joke around and waste my time again? *(All laugh)*
NEGAR:	Even if she does become Lame the way needed, Lame wouldn't marry her. *(The girl and the others laugh)*
NEXT GIRL:	*(Laughing)* You'll see, Negar.
SHAMAN:	OK. Enough. Sit down.

The girl sits down and Shaman takes a big syringe out of his bag.

SHAMAN:	Are you ready?
NEXT GIRL:	Yes.

Shaman puts the syringe into the back of her neck. Next girl screams with pain. Other girls cheer. Shaman, Friend and C.C. gather around her again.

SHAMAN:	Move your feet.
NEXT GIRL:	*(Unwell)* I can't. *(Shaman is thinking, and the others are silent.)* Did it work?

SHAMAN: We must see.... *(Hits the Girl with the big bludgeon and then inspects)* It didn't work. Next one. *(All the girls become happy)*

SCENE 4

Friend and Negar; By a waterfall or a fountain.

NEGAR: What exactly should I do?

FRIEND: I don't know. Anything you can.

NEGAR: I can do nothing.

FRIEND: I don't know. *(Desperately)* It seems there's no end to this island's problems.

NEGAR: Up until now, I haven't had any problems with this island.

FRIEND: First, that story of marrying and now, this new issue.

NEGAR: Trust me, I will do anything I can for this island.

FRIEND: I'm sure you will. That is why I came to you first.

NEGAR: *(Incredulously)* You mean no one else but us knows anything about this?

FRIEND: No one.

NEGAR: Even Shaman?

FRIEND: Even Shaman. Even C.C.. I didn't even tell my wife.

NEGAR:	I'm sure they'd do anything they could for the island.
FRIEND:	I told them nothing because of you.
NEGAR:	Because of me?
FRIEND:	If people realise what's happened, they'd blame you.
NEGAR:	But I have no guilt.
FRIEND:	I understand, but do you think Shaman or C.C. will understand this?
NEGAR:	Excuse me, but I think you don't understand it either.
FRIEND:	If I didn't, I wouldn't have come to you first.
NEGAR:	I'm sorry, but if you really understood, you wouldn't ask me such a thing.
FRIEND:	I came here to consult, or perhaps you can do something.
NEGAR:	Trust me, I still don't know what's happening. Please explain to me.
FRIEND:	He's fading. He is withering.

NEGAR:	You mean it's possible that… *(Doesn't continue)*	
FRIEND:	Yes… *(Negar becomes sad)* He will probably start to shrink in the next few days.	
NEGAR:	I swear on Lame's life I did not know. I really don't know what to do.	
FRIEND:	Neither do I.	
NEGAR:	Look. I'll do anything I can. My first priority is for Lame's welfare, then for myself and then for the people of the Island.	
FRIEND:	Yesterday I guessed something was happening.	
NEGAR:	Why yesterday?	
FRIEND:	When Lame suddenly cut the 'paralysing ceremony' for no apparent reason, it was not hard to understand why.	
NEGAR:	I was about to cry. I thought I had no chance.	
FRIEND:	Save your tears. It seems that our misery is not too far away.	
NEGAR:	My misery.	

FRIEND: People will realise everything if we don't make a decision soon.

NEGAR: They will realise anyway.

FRIEND: We can do something.

NEGAR: What?

FRIEND: It's the only way, I think.

NEGAR: And what is it?

FRIEND: Go to Lame and talk to him.

NEGAR: You think it will work?

FRIEND: Just do it before people find out. Otherwise they may blame you.

SCENE 5

People of the Island except Lame have gathered.

NEGAR: I thought it'd take at least a day before you became aware, but I was wrong.

C.C.: Anyway, this is a problem that you have made.

NEGAR: It's not a problem of my making.

SHAMAN: Maybe you're not the one to blame, but you can fix it.

NEGAR: I've said it once and I'll say it again, I always try to do my best, for Lame, myself and all people of the island, but I can't promise you anything.

SHAMAN: You're not in a situation to speak like this.

NEGAR: I can speak just like this in any situation.

C.C.: Look, Negar. We all talked before we came here, I think you should know what decision we made.

NEGAR: And...?

C.C.: We will ask you first.

SHAMAN:	Which I can clearly see, will not work.
C.C.:	Then I guess we'll have to threaten you.
SHAMAN:	Which we haven't done yet.
NEGAR:	This single sentence alone is enough for me to feel threatened.
C.C.:	If we don't get what we want, we'll have to, for Lame's sake, torture you.
NEGAR:	Why should you threaten or torture me?
FRIEND'S WIFE:	Because 'shrinking' starts in the next few days.
NEGAR:	*(To Friend)* Why don't you say something?
FRIEND:	What should I say?
NEGAR:	Tell these people.
FRIEND:	I warned you this morning.
NEGAR:	*(Angrily)* What the hell does your warning do for me? *(Friend shrugs his head)* It's not my fault. All girls on the island are in love with Lame. And I'm just one of them.

C.C.:	Now, you're different.
NEGAR:	I'm not different. I just fell in love with him. That's all. And it's something new. I was in love with him since my adolescence. Like all girls my age. Only perhaps more or less than others, maybe, I don't know.
C.C.:	I said now, you're different.
NEGAR:	How so?
C.C.:	Now, Lame is in love with you too. And this is a major difference.
SHAMAN:	And now, you have to do something about it.
NEGAR:	I'd make him mine, if I could, just as when I was a teenager. Believe me.
SHAMAN:	You know that's impossible.
NEGAR:	*(Sad and disappointed with speaking)* Why didn't he fall in love with me, when we were at school?
PARIA:	We don't know, but now, it's obvious what you should do.
NEGAR:	And what is that?

SHAMAN:	You should make Lame forget about your love.
NEGAR:	*(Suddenly realising)* Lame wants me to marry him, doesn't he?
SHAMAN:	Yes, he does.
NEGAR:	And you want me to do something against Lame's will?
SHAMAN:	*(Stammering)* Well… Ah… You… Should…
C.C.:	No, we would never want you to do such a thing.
NEGAR:	What then?
C.C.:	Anyway, it's not our problem. You should do something about it. Just remember not to do anything against Lame's will. *(Negar scoffs)*
FRIEND:	I think the only solution, is what I told you.
FRIEND'S WIFE:	What have you told her?
FRIEND:	I told her to go and speak with Lame.
PARIA:	Good idea.
FRIEND'S WIFE:	I agree.

C.C.:	So do I.
SHAMAN:	Isn't there any other solution?
FRIEND:	It seems not.
SHAMAN:	But that may possibly make it worse.
FRIEND:	There is no cure.
SHAMAN:	So then, I must agree.
C.C.:	Do you agree too, Negar?
NEGAR:	Can I not?
C.C.:	No.
NEGAR:	*(Smiles)* That's very kind of you.
SHAMAN:	Don't tell Lame that you were with us.
NEGAR:	If he asks?
SHAMAN:	Do not tell him what we have told you.

SCENE 6

Lame's place. Lame is lying down on his bed and seems very sick. His voice has changed a little and it is hard for him to talk.

FRIEND:	Haven't you got better?
LAME:	Negar didn't come?
FRIEND:	She will arrive soon.
LAME:	I miss her.
FRIEND:	Do you feel any pain in your stomach?
LAME:	Have the people found out yet?
FRIEND:	*(Trying to change the subject)* Shall I make some herbal tea for you?
LAME:	Herbal tea is not good for me. Have a look outside, see if she's arrived.
FRIEND:	*(Looking outside)* She'd knock when she arrives.
LAME:	Haven't people realised anything?
FRIEND:	They will, soon.
LAME:	Why?
FRIEND:	Your stature.

LAME:	Go ahead. Measure.

Friend measures the length of Lame. He is sad and says nothing.

LAME:	Well?
FRIEND:	You've shrunk about one centimetre.
LAME:	Do I look short to Negar?
FRIEND:	Not yet.
LAME:	Can you please do my hair?
FRIEND:	*(Combing)* This is pointless. All girls on the island are in love with you.
LAME:	What about Negar?
FRIEND:	She's a girl from this island as well.
LAME:	*(Smiles bitterly)* Anyway, it doesn't make any difference.
FRIEND:	Do you wish you were, normal?
LAME:	Never ask me that question again.
FRIEND:	Your hair's become a little curly here.
LAME:	How tall do you think Negar is?

Act II   Scene 6

FRIEND: I don't know. She might be about 170 centimetres.

Someone knocks.

FRIEND: I think she's here. I'll open the door then leave.

LAME: Am I well groomed?

FRIEND: Yes. Absolutely. Goodbye.

Friend exits, and Negar enters.

NEGAR: Hi.

LAME: Hi.

NEGAR: What's happened to you? *(Silence)*

LAME: *(Looks at Negar in silence)* That day of the 'paralysing', you were so sweet.

NEGAR: I really wanted you to be attracted to me.

LAME: There was no need.

NEGAR: That day, you were more handsome than ever, sir.

LAME: *(Quizzically)* You know me well.

NEGAR: You know me well too.

LAME:	Why 'Sir'?
NEGAR:	Because I've always wanted to call people sir.
LAME:	This 'always' won't last much...
NEGAR:	You haven't done your hair yourself, have you?
LAME:	How did you know?
NEGAR:	If you have watched someone for fifteen years, you learn how he does his hair.
LAME:	You don't think I've changed over that time?
NEGAR:	No.
LAME:	Honestly?
NEGAR:	Yes.
LAME:	I've become some centimetres shorter.
NEGAR:	I don't care, so neither should you.
LAME:	From now on, I'll become shorter and shorter.
NEGAR:	I don't care. I love you.
LAME:	Do you know why I'm shrinking?

NEGAR:	Yes.
LAME:	When a Lame falls in love, he starts shrinking day by day.
NEGAR:	If I knew you'd cut the 'paralysing ceremony' because of me, I'd be happy instead of crying. *(Long silence)*
LAME:	Yesterday, I was thinking that I'm so stupid.
NEGAR:	Why?
LAME:	I did not see you for such a long time.
NEGAR:	I saw enough for both of us. *(Long silence)*
LAME:	You know what I want?
NEGAR:	What?
LAME:	I want to take your hand for a moment, and I don't care what happens next.
NEGAR:	*(Crying)* If I was Lame, surely, I'd hug you now, put my head on your chest and cry.

LAME:	If you were Lame or I was normal, maybe we would not have fallen in love.
NEGAR:	Maybe. But you're not normal and I'm not Lame. *(Long silence)*
LAME:	*(Outstretches his hand toward Negar)* Will you take my hand, if I ask you to?
NEGAR:	I know you won't.
LAME:	And if I do?
NEGAR:	Even if it destroys the whole island, I'd do that. But you won't.
LAME:	The next time you come to see me, I will be much shorter.
NEGAR:	I pray not. *(Long silence)*
LAME:	I hope that after my death, no one will say how stupid was my death.
NEGAR:	I'm not like Paria.
LAME:	I'm sure you are not. When I'm dead, there will be no one to ask you to stop crying.
NEGAR:	I'm glad. *(Long silence)*
LAME:	May I request something of you?

NEGAR:	Anything.
LAME:	Cry very much over my death, very much. Dry all the trees of the island with the salinity of your tears.
NEGAR:	You have my word, sir.

Act III

SCENE 1

Shaman's place. Lame is much smaller, and his voice has changed even more. He looks very sick.

LAME: I can't read properly.

SHAMAN: Of course you can.

LAME: I don't feel good.

SHAMAN: Do you like what I'm going to talk about?

LAME: There's nothing I like anymore.

SHAMAN: Listen...

LAME: When I was a young boy, I never noticed Negar at school.

SHAMAN: Because you had to pay attention to the teacher.

LAME: Because I always had to sit in front of the class and she was always behind me.

SHAMAN: Because good students sit in front of the class.

LAME: Because I always thought that sitting there made me different.

SHAMAN:	Because you had to learn the lessons better than everyone else.
LAME:	Because in those days I didn't understand that I could ask for anything that I needed.
SHAMAN:	If you did know?
LAME:	If I knew, I would sit at the end of the class or in the middle, or anywhere else. Then maybe I would have seen Negar sooner.
SHAMAN:	I wish you had never seen her.
LAME:	Negar is a good girl.
SHAMAN:	*(Angrily)* Negar, Negar, Negar. When a man falls in love, he places his love so high that even he cannot reach her.
LAME:	Yes, they do.
SHAMAN:	You've put Negar somewhere in the clouds.
LAME:	It doesn't matter that she's in the clouds or next to my bed. I can't reach her anyway.
SHAMAN:	Bullshit.
LAME:	What?

Act III Scene 1

SHAMAN: This shit which has made you feel like this and say, 'I'm in love, I'm in love'.

LAME: It's not bullshit.

SHAMAN: Yes, it is. And its origin is from somewhere between your bellybutton to your knees.

It's not something strange or ethereal.

LAME: That's not true.

SHAMAN: So then how is it?

LAME: It's a love relationship that makes a Lame shrink. That's the time where he needs the most help.

Surely after me there'll be another Lame.

SHAMAN: I wish that Lame had been taught by a good Shaman, not to get crazy like you.

LAME: No Shaman can stop craziness.

SHAMAN:	A Shaman can do anything he wants. If you didn't stop me when I wanted to erase your love, I would've shown you how your craziness would disappear.
LAME:	I wish you'd understand what I'm saying.
SHAMAN:	I do understand.
LAME:	If you did, you'd not speak like this.
SHAMAN:	I speak like this because I do understand.
LAME:	*(Yells)* You don't understand love. You're just an old imbecile Shaman who just knows how to taunt.
SHAMAN:	*(Suddenly gets angry; Much more than Lame)* I'm not old and imbecile. I understand what love is. Long before you, idiot. I ate nothing but cookies for eighteen years because I was in love with a beautiful girl who is now a fat old woman; a fat old woman who just cries when she becomes lonely, for an old imbecile Shaman. *(Silence. Shaman rubs his eyes but doesn't cry.)*
LAME:	I'm sorry, I had no idea.

SHAMAN:	Forget it.
LAME:	C.C.?
SHAMAN:	I told you, to forget it.
LAME:	Answer me.
SHAMAN:	Yes. Let's just continue the lesson.
LAME:	What happened between you two?
SHAMAN:	It's not important.
LAME:	Tell me.
SHAMAN:	We were supposed to get married but it never happened.
LAME:	You still love her?
SHAMAN:	And she loves me too.
LAME:	*(Shocked)* Then what happened?
SHAMAN:	Things went, wrong.
LAME:	Don't you want to tell me?
SHAMAN:	No.
LAME:	What if I ask you two to return to each other?
SHAMAN:	Please don't do this to me.
LAME:	Read my will after my death.

SHAMAN:	It's been forty years. It's over. Don't open old wounds.
LAME:	If after forty years it's still true, it has never been finished.
SHAMAN:	Do you want me to beg?
LAME:	There's no need.
SHAMAN:	So, do not speak about your will ever again.
LAME:	I didn't say I was going to order you to get married in my will.
SHAMAN:	What then?
LAME:	You'll find out when you read my will.

SCENE 2

C.C.'s place. C.C. is making cookies for herself, Friend's wife and Paria.

C.C.: Believe me, he was not a good husband.

PARIA: I don't know what to say.

FRIEND'S WIFE: She still loves him.

PARIA: Well we did live three or four years together. Of course I'm still thinking of him.

C.C.: Well, you shouldn't. Let him go.

FRIEND'S WIFE: Don't blame her.

C.C.: You miss him?

PARIA: Yes. Very much.

C.C.: *(Happy)* I see. Oh, that's enough. Let it go. Don't get sad.

PARIA: I'm not.

FRIEND'S WIFE: Aren't you?

PARIA: No.

FRIEND'S WIFE: Why not?

PARIA:	Lame told me not to be sad. Don't you remember?
C.C.:	That's good.
FRIEND'S WIFE:	Why do you insist that he was no good for Paria?
C.C.:	*(Smiles shrewdly)* Because I have a plan for her.
FRIEND'S WIFE:	*(Also smiles shrewdly)* OK, so you have a plan for her...
PARIA:	No. It's not a good time.
C.C.:	You only have to see him. You don't have to go out with him.
PARIA:	The man I loved, died for me, and you expect me to get married so soon?
C.C.:	I just said see him. Then we'll talk.

C.C. points to Friend's wife, then to a man passing the window. Friend's wife sees him, and unknown to both Paria sees him also.

FRIEND'S WIFE:	*(To C.C.)* The one you showed me the other day?
C.C.:	Yes.

FRIEND'S WIFE:	*(To Paria)* Tall, handsome, I think you'll like him.
PARIA:	*(Pretends not to care)* Who is he, by the way?
FRIEND'S WIFE:	*(Smiles)* You naughty girl. You have noticed him.
C.C.:	He was walking along the coast alone yesterday.
PARIA:	*(Trying to change the subject)* Anyway, what's the news about Negar?
C.C.:	OK, we'll change the subject, shall we?
PARIA:	No, I really mean it.
C.C.:	You know the whole story. Nothing new.
PARIA:	Couldn't she do anything?
FRIEND'S WIFE:	No. She's even worse than Lame.
PARIA:	Why?
FRIEND'S WIFE:	Every time she sees Lame, she says she's going to die from pleasure.
PARIA:	The day of 'paralysing' she became so sugary sweet.

FRIEND'S WIFE:	Yes, that long-legged girl really wanted to attract him.
PARIA:	I think she was a little gaudy.
C.C.:	I think I can safely say, so were you once before.
PARIA:	*(Smiles with shame)* Well, what could I do?
C.C.:	You're right. You were lucky that it wasn't your turn.
PARIA:	I wish he'd stopped the ceremony after Negar's turn.
C.C.:	When he realised that 'paralysing' doesn't work, he cut the ceremony so as not to hurt his dear Negar.
FRIEND'S WIFE:	You mean it? Seriously?
PARIA:	He's becoming smaller every day because of her. Don't you see?
C.C.:	We should do something about Negar. It shouldn't be like this.
PARIA:	I agree.
FRIEND'S WIFE:	Why? It's not her fault, anyway.
C.C.:	I don't know what to say.

SCENE 3

Shaman's place. Magic and sorcery accessories are seen all around the room. Negar is sitting strapped to a chair and looks torpid. Shaman's movements are demoniac.

SHAMAN: I told you it might come to this.

NEGAR: *(Doesn't want to speak)* I cannot do anything.

SHAMAN: Lame has become so small now.

NEGAR: Can't you do something with all your powers? If you can't what could I possibly do?

SHAMAN: When you came here, you didn't believe I could do this to you, did you?

NEGAR: No.

SHAMAN: Tell that stupid lover of yours not to call me an old imbecile.

NEGAR: I will, I will.

SHAMAN: Tell him that he killed me with a wave of his hand.

Moves his hand and Negar dies. Silence.

And then he resurrected me with another wave.

Moves his hand again and Negar comes back to life

NEGAR: *(Crying)* You've said that a thousand times. Trust me, I will tell him.

SHAMAN: Tell him I did this many times.

NEGAR: I said I will. Let me go, Shaman. Please.

SHAMAN: Lame's going to die in a few days, do you understand?

NEGAR: *(Angry and crying)* I told you, he doesn't accept it.

SHAMAN: Don't you raise your voice to me.

NEGAR: *(Angry)* I'll tell him. I'll tell him what you did to me. You'll see.

SHAMAN: Shut up. *(Moves his hands and Negar dies with pain)*

Do you want me to not bring you back next time, huh? Would you like to remain dead like this? *(Moves his hand and Negar comes back to life again.)*

Act III   Scene 3

NEGAR: *(Laughing)* If you do this to me another thousand times, I still will not do anything for you.

SHAMAN: *(Surprised)* What?

NEGAR: You know what? I can do something that will force him to forget about my love. But I won't. I won't.

SHAMAN: *(Yelling)* Shut up.

NEGAR: Because I love him. I'm in love with him.

SHAMAN: *(Trying to look dispassionate)* You can't do anything, bitch.

NEGAR: A 'bitch' is someone who prefers a dead-drunk guy over her own man. One sad night instead of eighteen years. Lame's told me everything. You've had your fun.

Shaman is shocked. He stares at Negar. He slumps to the ground and starts crying.

SHAMAN: I knew he'd tell you. Negar, I beg you not to tell this to anyone.

NEGAR: He told me because he wanted to help you.

SHAMAN:	If he wanted to help me, he'd have simply asked C.C..
NEGAR:	He didn't want it to be this way.
SHAMAN:	Negar, I beg you not to say anything to anyone.
NEGAR:	In the last hour you killed me and then resurrect me at least five times. Now, look at you. Where is your power now, you old imbecile Shaman?
SHAMAN:	There are moments when even a Shaman gets crushed.
NEGAR:	*(Trying to hurt Shaman)* He gets crushed so much that after forty years he goes to his ex-love and begs her to come back, but she ignores him.
SHAMAN:	How did you know that?
NEGAR:	Remember that I am Lame's lover.
SHAMAN:	*(Yelling)* You bitch. *(Moves his hand and Negar dies)*

SCENE 4

Friend's place. Friend and his wife are cooking.

FRIEND: That's enough. Stop it.

FRIEND'S WIFE: I didn't say anything.

FRIEND: Anyway, it doesn't matter.

FRIEND'S WIFE: I just...

FRIEND: *(Interrupts her)* I said it's in the past and it doesn't matter. I don't want to talk about it.

FRIEND'S WIFE: OK, dear.

FRIEND: I don't even want to think about it.

FRIEND'S WIFE: I said OK. I won't continue.

FRIEND: Do not continue. I want to forget it.

FRIEND'S WIFE: OK. Anything you wish.

FRIEND: Good.

FRIEND'S WIFE: You know? It's really good that we're doing everything for Lame all by ourselves.

FRIEND: People are shallow. Since Lame's started to shrink, no one does anything for him anymore.

FRIEND'S WIFE: I don't know. But people from the island don't appear to be normal. Something's wrong with them.

FRIEND: What is wrong with them?

FRIEND'S WIFE: Shaman has all but disappeared. We only see him around occasionally nowadays. I haven't seen him at all during last four or five days.

FRIEND: Yes. I don't know where he has been going.

FRIEND'S WIFE: Surely he's been working on some new magic.

FRIEND: Maybe he's making some new spell for Lame.

FRIEND'S WIFE: I don't think so. Because Lame's asked him to help stop his shrinking.

FRIEND: Good.

FRIEND'S WIFE: C.C. doesn't talk at all. I don't know why she's become so sad all of a sudden.

Act III Scene 4   91

FRIEND: Let them do what they want. When Lame was healthy, they always took food for him and ingratiated themselves before him. But now, everyone's gone.

FRIEND'S WIFE: I don't think so. Something's wrong with them.

FRIEND: Shaman and C.C. have issues, what about the others?

FRIEND'S WIFE: Who do you mean?

FRIEND: What about Paria?

FRIEND'S WIFE: Do not mention her name. I don't like her at all.

FRIEND: Why? Has something happened?

FRIEND'S WIFE: I just don't like her.

FRIEND: Why?

FRIEND'S WIFE: She's been seeing a guy and fallen for him. C.C. introduced her.

FRIEND: Take it easy. It's none of our business.

FRIEND'S WIFE: Did you ask Lame if he's satisfied with the meals?

FRIEND: Who doesn't like your cooking?

FRIEND'S WIFE:	*(Smiling)* Thanks. Didn't he ask for something special?
FRIEND:	No. He's satisfied. He just asked for less lime.
FRIEND'S WIFE:	But it was he who asked me to pour the lime over the food.
FRIEND:	He's not wrong. You pour lime over everything you cook: soup, cutlets, barbecue...
FRIEND'S WIFE:	OK, I won't anymore. No one else has come to see him?
FRIEND:	Yes, some people were there yesterday. You have no idea how good it was when he said I should be the only one to bring him food.
FRIEND'S WIFE:	I wish I was there too.
FRIEND:	But then he ruined the moment. After people left, he said he's sick and doesn't want to eat 'different' meals.
FRIEND'S WIFE:	Maybe he doesn't want to hurt Shaman and the others.
FRIEND:	Maybe. Hurry up. I have to go.
FRIEND'S WIFE:	It's almost ready. It'll be finished while you're getting dressed.

SCENE 5

Lame's place. Lame's become a thirty-centimetre creature who is kept in a glass box and can hardly talk.

LAME:	I can't do my hair anymore.
NEGAR:	Forget about it. It's beautiful just as is.
LAME:	I can hardly breathe. My throat's dry.
NEGAR:	You want some water?
LAME:	My right shoulder aches.
NEGAR:	What can I do?
LAME:	I want to get out of this glass box.
NEGAR:	Shall I do that?
LAME:	Yes. Take me out of this box.
NEGAR:	*(Hesitates)* Well… then I will have to take your hand.
LAME:	But we can't.
NEGAR:	Can I do anything else then?
LAME:	Are you sad that I'm dying?
NEGAR:	No.
LAME:	No?

NEGAR:	You're still alive, and by my side, and still talking to me. Why should I be sad?
LAME:	Don't I look disgusting?
NEGAR:	*(Smiles)* I think you are not well.
LAME:	I'm OK now.
NEGAR:	Good.
LAME:	Don't forget to cry for me when I am gone?
NEGAR:	*(Laughing)* Trust me. I'll do my very best for you. I'll cry so much until I am unconscious. OK?
LAME:	Perfect.
NEGAR:	So be happy. Laugh.
LAME:	I can't.
NEGAR:	Laugh. Please.
LAME:	I am a thirty-centimetre Lame who's dying. Do you think I can laugh?
NEGAR:	Yes, you can. Laugh for Negar's sake.

Lame makes a sound like laughter. Negar laughs.

NEGAR:	(Laughing) What was that?

Act III   Scene 5

LAME: A laugh.

NEGAR: Very funny.

LAME: I've written a will and put it under my bed. After my death, take it out and read it to the people.

NEGAR: Can I read it now?

LAME: No. I'm still alive. Read it after my death.

NEGAR: OK then. What've you written in it?

LAME: It's not that important. Just remember, read it in the presence of Shaman.

NEGAR: Sure.

LAME: Know that I've written a few things about him and C.C. in it.

NEGAR: I don't speak to Shaman. You make sure he comes that day.

LAME: Why don't you speak to him?

NEGAR: He doesn't deserve your favour.

LAME: How do you know I want to do him a favour?

NEGAR:	When you say you've written about him and C.C., it's quite obvious that you're going to do him a favour.
LAME:	I didn't say what I've written, did I?
NEGAR:	He deserves anything bad that you'd do to him.
LAME:	It is neither good nor bad.
NEGAR:	What is it then?
LAME:	Why don't you speak to Shaman?
NEGAR:	Because he was trying to do something that would make you forget about my love.
LAME:	He hurt you?
NEGAR:	Very much.
LAME:	I don't want to demand anything of you, it's just a question.
	Could you forgive him if I ask you to?
NEGAR:	Do you think it would be any another way if you asked?
LAME:	I've not asked you anything yet.
NEGAR:	Anything it is. I'll do it, sir.

Act III   Scene 5

LAME: So, forgive him, for me.

NEGAR: OK. *(Silence)* Don't look at me that way.

LAME: I'm about to die. Which way should I look at you?

NEGAR: Any way but this way.

LAME: What way is this?

NEGAR: Desperately.

LAME: It shouldn't be so?

NEGAR: No.

LAME: *(Smiles)* I always look at people desperately when I'm desperate.

NEGAR: Have some hope.

LAME: How? I will be dead in a few days.

NEGAR: I have hope.

LAME: Really?

NEGAR: Yes.

LAME: Why?

NEGAR: I'm thinking that if you get much smaller, there'd be nothing left of you. You might be born again like phoenix. Or perhaps via your shrinking, you might suddenly change into something else, like a swan, perhaps. Then I can have you to myself once again.

LAME: What would you do with a swan?

NEGAR: It doesn't matter. It would be you.

LAME: Let me tell you. I won't be reborn like phoenix. I won't change into a swan. I'll just get smaller, even smaller than this, and then one day, there'll be nothing left of me. On that day I will be dead.

SCENE 6

The same place of the first scene. It is a funeral, and everyone is present but Lame. They all are dressed in black and eating. Paria is seen beside her new husband.

FRIEND:	Great Shaman, what should we do now?
SHAMAN:	I really don't know.
C.C.:	Who else should know but Shaman?
SHAMAN:	Any funeral that I've ever held, has had a dead body. This is the first time that I'm in such a situation.
NEGAR:	It's not important what to do. It's enough that you've come here to pay respect to Lame.
SHAMAN:	There's no other way.
FRIEND'S WIFE:	*(Crying)* That's it? Now we just go home? This is all we could do for Lame?
FRIEND:	We can't do anything more, darling. We all did what we could.
FRIEND'S WIFE:	What did you do, for example?

C.C.:	I agree with her. I think we should do something more.
FRIEND:	I agree too.
SHAMAN:	So do I.
PARIA:	So do we.
C.C.:	I'll make some cookies and distribute it among the people for him.
SHAMAN:	And I will try to find a special rite for Lames.
FRIEND:	We've decided to take Negar on a holiday to make Lame's soul happy and to get Negar away from this sad situation. Of course, only if Negar accepts.
NEGAR:	No, now is not a good time.
FRIEND:	Why not? It'd be fun.
FRIEND'S WIFE:	He's right.
NEGAR:	Shall we discuss it later?
FRIEND:	I agree.

Act III   Scene 6

PARIA:	*(Pointing at herself and her new husband)* We've decided to postpone our marriage for seven months in respect for Lame's death.
SHAMAN:	*(Sarcastically)* It's very thoughtful of you.
	Anyway, I think it is time for us to read Lame's will.
C.C.:	I agree.
PARIA:	Don't you want to wait a few days?
FRIEND'S WIFE:	Look who's talking.
PARIA:	What have I done?
FRIEND'S WIFE:	Nothing.
PARIA:	Is it wrong to get married?
FRIEND'S WIFE:	It's not wrong, but not so soon.
PARIA:	I just said, I've postponed it.
FRIEND'S WIFE:	I want nothing to do with your marriage. Just let it be some time later.
PARIA:	Eight years ago, when you…

C.C.:	*(Interrupts her)* Paria. That's enough. This is not a good time. And I'm talking to the both of you.
SHAMAN:	She's right. It's time for the will.
FRIEND:	Where is the will?
SHAMAN:	I don't know.
C.C.:	I don't have it neither.
PARIA:	You don't expect me to know, do you?
FRIEND:	Negar?
NEGAR:	*(She has been distracted and has been silent. Startled.)* What?
FRIEND:	Do you know anything about the will?
NEGAR:	The will? Why?
SHAMAN:	We need to read it.
NEGAR:	Wills are to be read after people's death…
FRIEND:	What's the matter with you?
NEGAR:	Nothing. I was just lost in thought.
SHAMAN:	And what have you concluded?

Act III Scene 6

NEGAR: Something.

C.C.: So, tell us.

NEGAR: Yesterday morning, when I went to Lame's place, he wasn't there in his box. I thought perhaps he'd been sleeping in his bed. I removed his blanket, but he wasn't there either. I searched everywhere. He wasn't anywhere to be found.

SHAMAN: So?

NEGAR: He was just, not there. Can anyone prove he's actually dead?

FRIEND'S WIFE: I agree with her. *(They all look at Friend's wife)*

SHAMAN: Lame was going to get smaller and smaller, so much so that there'd be nothing left of him. He told us he would be dead by then.

NEGAR: When he drank pomegranate juice, he'd lose his hair. When he ate cream, his hair would grow back, and a thousand other weird things would happen to him. He was never predictable. Am I right?

SHAMAN: What are you getting at?

NEGAR: Maybe, we will be surprised one more time. Maybe, he's just gone, not dead.

SHAMAN: Anyway, we should read the will now.

NEGAR: Anyway, I have the will and I'm not going to give it to anyone.

C.C.: You can't do this.

NEGAR: Yes, I can. And I'll face the consequences. Am I right, Shaman?

SHAMAN: You've gone crazy.

NEGAR: I think he's still alive, he's just left this island, maybe he's gone to another island.

CURTAIN

Recommended Reading

Great works of Persian Ghazal poetry:

Divan-e-**Hafez**,

Rumi; Maṭnawīye Ma'nawī *(Spiritual Couplets)*, Dīwān-e Kabīr

Saadi; Bustan and Gulistan

Attar; Dīwān, Manṭiq-uṭ-Ṭayr also known as Ma-qāmāt-uṭṬ-Ṭuyūr *(A story about the birds falling in love)*

www.ingramcontent.com/pod-product-compliance
Lightning Source LLC
Chambersburg PA
CBHW070432010526
44118CB00014B/2006